Building With Machines

by Becky Manfredini

HOUGHTON MIFFLIN HARCOURT

PHOTOGRAPHY CREDITS: COVER ©Gallo Images/Getty Images; 4 (b) ©Corbis/SuperStock; 6 (t) ©wusuowei/Fotolia; 7 (br) ©Roman Milert/Alamy; 8 (br) ©gilles lougassi/Fotolia; 9 (tr) ©Universal Images Group/Getty Images; 10 (tr) ©George Doyle/Stockbyte/Getty Images; 12 (b) ©Flickr RF/Getty Images; 13 (tr) ©Gallo Images/Getty Images

Printed in U.S.A.

ISBN: 978-0-544-07294-7

3 4 5 6 7 8 9 10 1083 21 20 19 18 17 16 15 14

4500470116   A B C D E F G

Contents

Vocabulary

work

simple machine

inclined plane

force

pulley

lever

fulcrum

wedge

screw

compound machine

gravity

weight

wheel-and-axle

Stretch Vocabulary

hydraulic

caisson

excavate

Introduction

Throughout the world, you can look around and see buildings, bridges, and walls. People and machines built each structure. Some of these structures are from times long ago. Others are modern, built in the past 100 years.

Pause and think about how these amazing structures were built. Maybe they will inspire you to think about something you would like to build. What machines would *you* use to build a structure?

Old, new, and somewhere in-between, which of these structures is your favorite? Read on to find out!

This toy parking structure uses machines. Can you find the machines?

Great Pyramid

Work is done when a push or a pull has been used to move something. Is lifting a stone that weighs a few tons work? A scientist would say yes!

About 4,500 years ago, ancient Egyptians built pyramids to protect the tombs of pharaohs, or kings. Today, people continue to marvel at how the Egyptians built the Great Pyramid without using modern machines.

Scientists and historians think that it took twenty years, 100,000 people, many animals, and some simple machines to build the Great Pyramid. A simple machine is a tool with few or no moving parts. With a lot of hard work and sweat, the workers and animals pushed and pulled the pyramid's stones into place. The workers used a simple machine to help them.

The Great Pyramid was once about 147 meters (481 feet) tall. How do you think workers put the last stone on top?

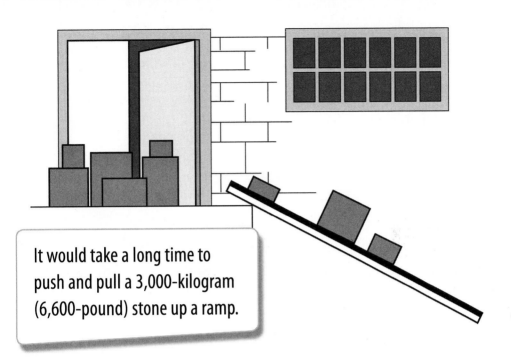

It would take a long time to push and pull a 3,000-kilogram (6,600-pound) stone up a ramp.

Historians and scientists still wonder how the Great Pyramid was built. Many think that the Egyptians used inclined planes called ramps to build it. An inclined plane is a simple machine that has a slanted surface. Egyptian workers probably made the ramps out of mud bricks.

Scientists and historians think that Egyptians used wooden sleds and ropes to push and pull the stones up the ramps. The workers piled the stones on top of each other to build the pyramid.

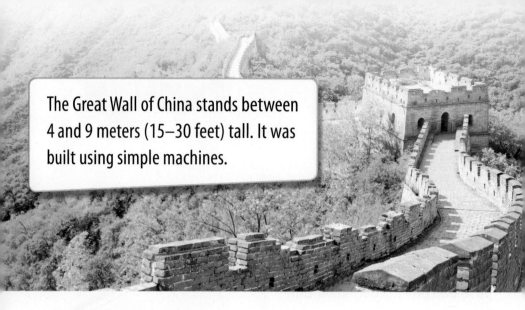

The Great Wall of China stands between 4 and 9 meters (15–30 feet) tall. It was built using simple machines.

Great Wall of China

The Great Wall of China is about 8,900 km (5,500 miles) long and snakes along hills and through deserts. This engineering wonder took about 2,000 years to build. Most of the wall is human-made. Workers used earth, grass, stone, wood, and brick to build it.

Chinese workers used simple machines to make the construction of the Great Wall easier. They used a pulley along the wall to lift up baskets filled with stones. A pulley is a simple machine made of a wheel with a rope around it. Ends of the rope hang on both sides of the pulley. The load is connected to one end. By pulling the other end of the rope, the load is raised.

Chinese workers used levers, such as crowbars, to move rocks. A lever is a simple machine made up of a bar that pivots, or turns, on a fixed point. The fixed point on a lever is called the fulcrum. As a worker pushed down one end of the crowbar, the other end lifted a heavy rock.

Workers also combined a hammer, another kind of lever, with a wedge. A wedge is two inclined planes back to back. The workers pounded the wedge with a hammer to crush stones to build the wall. A knife or an ax is another wedge. When an ax cuts, the blade splits an object.

A pulley is a simple machine made of a wheel with a rope around it.

load

A crowbar is a simple machine called a lever. A lever's fulcrum is its fixed point.

Eiffel Tower

Another amazing landmark is the Eiffel Tower! It was completed in 1889. Alexandre-Gustave Eiffel designed this 300-meter (1,000-foot) wrought-iron structure.

Workers first dug a foundation, or base, into the ground. The legs of the tower were secured by bolts, or screws. A screw is a simple machine made of a post with an inclined plane wrapped around it. Engineers used bolts to hold the tower's legs in place.

Workers used other machines to build the Eiffel Tower. A hydraulic jack, a water-fed machine, raised and lowered the tower's platforms. This compound machine used two simple machines, a lever and inclined plane.

Today the tower is about 23 meters (77 feet) taller than when it was built because of the addition of television towers.

Cranes lifted materials up to the platforms. Cranes could also move objects horizontally. These compound machines used levers and a pulley system to lift the tower's materials.

Workers added several elevators to the Eiffel Tower. The original elevators were hydraulic. Some of these elevators are still used today, while electric elevators replaced others. The glass-walled elevators use a pulley system. On one side of the pulley is a metal rope. On the other side is a heavy weight used to balance the car.

A hydraulic jack is a compound machine that combines a lever and inclined plane.

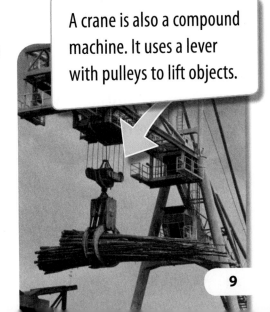

A crane is also a compound machine. It uses a lever with pulleys to lift objects.

Golden Gate Bridge

In the 1930s engineers built one of the most famous landmarks in the United States—the Golden Gate Bridge, which spans San Francisco Bay. This suspension bridge was built using massive steel cables to hold up the road. Workers draped the cables over two large towers that were anchored, or secured, in tons of concrete blocks. Work crews placed a safety net under the workers.

The Golden Gate Bridge was built to last even through earthquakes.

Engineers knew the bridge was going to be difficult to build. It had to withstand high winds, tides, and even earthquakes!

To make the bridge stable, workers built piers, or supports, at each end.

Workers built the north tower's pier on a ledge of bedrock found 6 meters (20 feet) below the water. The engineers needed to work 30 meters (100 feet) underwater to build the other pier. They constructed a large caisson, or airtight chamber, the size of a football field! They used a machine to pump out the water. After engineers had removed the water, they pumped in hundreds of tons of concrete to build the pier.

During construction of the towers, workers hammered approximately 600,000 metal rivets, or bolts, in each tower! The rivets held together heavy steel plates.

Workers painted the bridge orange so that ships could see it in the heavy fog that rolls in over the bay.

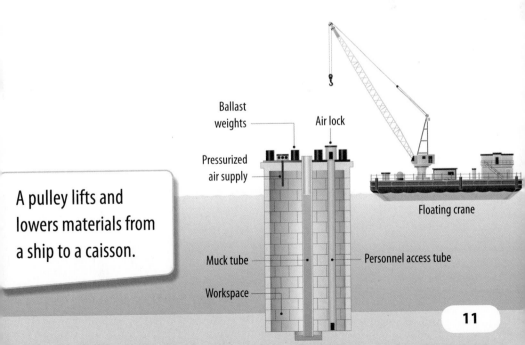

Ballast weights

Air lock

Pressurized air supply

A pulley lifts and lowers materials from a ship to a caisson.

Floating crane

Muck tube

Personnel access tube

Workspace

Skyscraper: Burj Khalifa

A skyscraper called Burj Khalifa is the tallest building in the world. It opened in 2010 in the city of Dubai, in the United Arab Emirates.

The building has 162 floors and is 828 meters (2,717 feet) high. The main concern in building a skyscraper is the downward pull of gravity. Gravity is a force that pulls objects toward Earth's center.

To construct a building that is 162 stories high, more structure needed to be on the bottom to support the weight of the upper floors. Weight is a measure of the force of gravity on an object. The foundation is made of concrete. A three-story platform was built to hold the tower in place.

Many modern compound machines were used to build this skyscraper.

Tower cranes are put together by smaller cranes, so these giant cranes are not able to move from place to place.

On the ground, many machines excavated, or dug out, a large hole to make room for the foundation. Trucks used to move materials have another kind of simple machine. A wheel-and-axle consists of a wheel and an axle that are connected so that they turn together. When a worker turns the machine's steering wheel, the axle turns, too.

Tower cranes made of steel lifted the heaviest loads. Once the main tower was complete, workers built the spire, or point, inside the tower. Then a hydraulic pump lifted it up and placed it at the top.

People and machines worked together to build this amazing structure!

Build a Simple Machine

Think about the six kinds of simple machines you read about. Choose one and draw a diagram of it. Label your picture. Underneath your diagram, write an explanation of how it works. Using materials in your classroom, make a model of your simple machine. Gather classmates around you, then demonstrate how to use it.

Write About It!

Choose a building, bridge, or structure that you find interesting. Using the Internet or other resources, research the machines used to construct it or machines that operate it. Draw a picture of the structure and write a report about it. Share this information with the class.

Glossary

caisson [KAY•suhn] An airtight chamber used in construction work under water.

compound machine [KOM•pound muh•SHEEN] A machine that is made up of two or more simple machines.

excavate [EKS•kuh•vayt] To dig out by removing material.

force [FOHRS] A push or a pull.

fulcrum [FUHL•kruhm] The balance point of a lever that supports the arm but does not move.

gravity [GRAV•i•tee] A force that pulls two objects toward each other.

hydraulic [hy•DRAW•lik] Operated by the pressure of water in motion.

inclined plane [in•KLYND PLAYN] A simple machine that is a slanted surface.

lever [LEV•er] A simple machine made up of a bar that pivots, or turns, on a fixed point.

pulley [PUHL·ee] A simple machine made of a wheel with a rope, cord, or chain around it.

screw [SKROO] A simple machine made of a post with an inclined plane wrapped around it.

simple machine [SIM·puhl muh·SHEEN] A machine with few or no moving parts that you apply just one force to.

wedge [WEJ] A simple machine composed of two inclined planes back to back.

weight [WAYT] A measure of the force of gravity on an object.

wheel-and-axle [WEEL AND AK·suhl] A simple machine made of a wheel and an axle that turn together.

work [WERK] The use of a force to move an object over a distance.